Air Raids on Yardley

KEY TO FRONT AND BACK COVER

Blue circle = HE Bombs
Blue cross = Unexploded bombs
Red circle = Incendiary bombs
Red cross = Unexploded Incendiary
T= Crashed planes

See also maps on pages 50 - 53

Raiders Past
Air Raids on Yardley

by

John V. Abbott

BREWIN BOOKS

First published
by Brewin Books, Studley, Warwickshire, B80 7LG
in May 1993

British Library Cataloguing in Publication Data.
A Catalogue record for this book is available from the British Library

ISBN 1 85858 019 6

**Typeset by Avon Dataset, Bidford on Avon, Warwickshire, B50 4JH
and made and printed by Supaprint (Redditch) Limited. Redditch.**

Contents

The history of the ARP, as experienced at one Post by one individual, writing almost immediately after the events described.

Editor's Preface

This account was written by my father, John Vincent Abbott (1900-1985) shortly after the end of the war, using the official log books, of which – as Post Warden – he had been in charge, as well as other sources. The account was written in notebooks, in longhand, with many insertions, alterations and additions. Although completed, no fair copy was written, nor was any attempt apparently made to have the account printed. Indeed, my first knowledge of the existence of the notebooks came when my father gave them to me, some thirty years later. I have made no alterations or additions to the text, but I have put everything in the proper order, edited it where necessary and made a very small number of corrections. The account contains no dramatic events or new revelations, but it is a valuable and rare record of one of the smaller sideshows of the Second World War, now almost completely forgotten.

Patrick Abbott 1993

Preface

This booklet has been written to help to preserve, in the minds of the Air Raid Wardens attached to Post E.24A, some of the memories which might otherwise be forgotten.

No specific names have been mentioned but whilst not complete, everything recorded is true, though in some instance the reports have been much abbreviated.

It is not pretended that E.24A did not escape lightly compared with many other Wardens' Posts, but at least, it, too, had its nights!

Eight sectors – 17 roads – 1,120 houses – 5,182 approximate population.

Birmingham was divided into 9 divisions, comprising 37 sub-divisions. In all, there were 2,303 Sectors, and by 1942, 422 Wardens' Posts had been established, when the number of whole-time Wardens was 1,365 and voluntary part-time Wardens numbered 17,864.

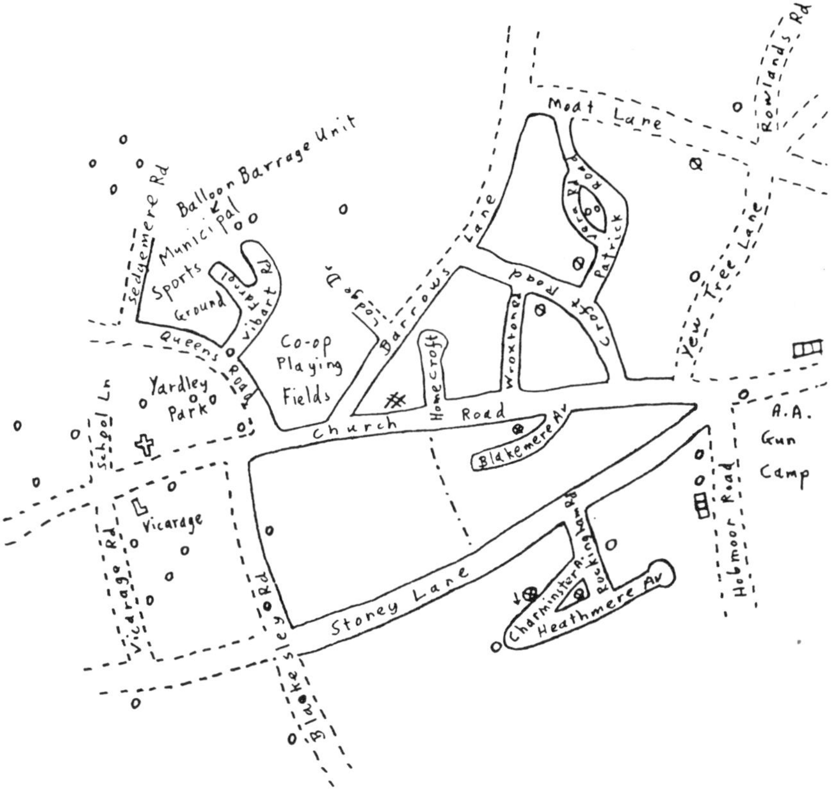

———	Post E.24A area
– – –	other areas
✝	Yardley church
#	Post E.24A
□□□	Schools

○ —— H.E. Bomb

⊖ —— D.A. Bomb

⊕ —— Oil Bomb

In addition, numerous incendiary bombs of all descriptions were dropped in all the roads, and in most of them, on more than one occasion.

John Abbott

Duty Memories

To most of even the Wardens attached to Post E.24A, its beginning is wrapped in mystery. However, when the Air Raid Wardens' Service was created in 1937, there responded to the call only two or three men from the area which afterwards came to be divided into the eight sections controlled from Post E.24A. After a few months the number of Wardens increased, but not to any great extent, and looking back, it is hard to reconstruct these early days when many an undesirable task was undertaken.

There was the great Gas Mask Issue, when the public was requested to attend at certain depots (in this case, the old Talbot Inn, in Church Road) to receive, and to be fitted with respirators. The gigantic task was undertaken by a few Wardens with the help of a small number of volunteers. Some months afterwards, came the Gas Mask Census, when a handful of Wardens visited every house, recorded particulars of the occupiers, fitted and adjusted respirators, gave advice, and issued cards to those whose masks required changing or who had no masks at all. Many refused to be interviewed through obstinacy or fear, or because they had no time to waste, or it was 'something that would never be required'.

Many would not test their respirators, vowing they would never be able to breathe whilst wearing them, and they were assured the time might come when they would not be able to breathe without wearing them! Masks were not then available for babies and small children, and consequently fond parents had not the slightest interest in their own respirators.

The work of the Wardens at that time, as ever after, was a thankless job which required patience, tact, diplomacy and often the temper of a saint. During this period, even the weather was against the little band of Wardens, for with heavy falls of snow, it was no wonder that they were sometimes forced to ask to be allowed to enter dwellings, rather than to attempt to fit the family on the doorstep.

Many months afterwards, the census was retaken and masks and helmets were issued to small children and babies. Even later still – during those dark days of June 1940 – a 'contex' had to be attached to every gas mask and the public was requested to attend at the Post, where the Wardens worked until blisters appeared on already strained fingers.

After the first few days of the War, the Post was established in a garage (or rather a converted stable) at the corner of Church Road and Blakesley Road, where there was still a motor car, one small window, no means of heating, and a door which necessitated the light being extinguished each time it was opened. The atmosphere was not to be likened to the Blackpool air and the only telephone available was in the owner's house, nearby.

In those first few black weeks when one knew not what to expect, the Wardens patrolled the roads each night, a fact unknown to the great majority of the citizens in their beds. Looking back, one wonders why all this was thought to be necessary – the eerie darkness of the now unlighted roads was a new experience, but all this was often enlightened by a sense of humour.

There was the night when the electric current failed in the locality, and Wardens were quickly reassuring members of the public who had appeared hastily at their front doors in night attire, fearing Hitler's secret weapon would suddenly switch them away into an awful unknown.

How many tales could be told of the experience of the now ever-increasing band of Wardens who nightly patrolled the area asking or demanding that lights should be better screened? It was discovered that the public was either scared of the Warden or thought him an object to be insulted. A civilian with a yellow armlet, and (if lucky) a 'tin hat' was no doubt a figure which offered a chance to relieve the feelings of the overwrought.

Mock air-raids, or exercises, were held and 'incidents' were dropped in the form of notes in sealed envelopes from motor cars to waiting Wardens. The latter had then to make out a report in the approved style and see that it was immediately transmitted to a spot deemed, for the occasion, to be the Report Centre. On one of these exercises, a real fire was started, but owing to a 'technical hitch' the A.F.S. arrived at the scene of the incident only just in time to extinguish the conflagration before 'black-out' time!

There was also the incident where an imaginary delayed action bomb was 'dropped' at a cross roads, and a super-conscientious Warden sent in his report and then diverted all the traffic from the imaginary danger spot, much to the astonishment and bewilderment of pedestrians and motorists. As the hour-hand of his watch told him the exercise was over, he immediately entered his house (which was opposite the 'crater') leaving the public unenlightened!

It was at about this time that the new Post at 332 Church Road had been secured, complete with telephone and furniture, in which a gas fire (with ring) was eventually fixed, and two beds installed. This was indeed a palace compared with the slum of the Post evacuated. The permanent Wardens found there comparative comfort, notwithstanding that they lived in a practically perpetual blackout, as it was thought necessary to erect a wall of sand bags outside the window.

For the first few months it was considered advisable for at least two voluntary Wardens to be always available during the nights, so that immediate warning could be given on whistles in case of enemy activity in the neighbourhood. Consequently, each night from 10 p.m. to 2 a.m. voluntary Wardens were at the post along with their two paid colleagues and at 2 a.m. they were relieved by more voluntary Wardens, who stayed until 6 a.m. It was during this period that many a Warden learnt the intricacies of solo whist, auction bridge, draughts, chess, and even the Shakespearean game of Nine Men Morris was resurrected. Although this practice ceased after a short while, it was (periodically) revised on the nights of Saturday-Sunday to enable the full-time Warden to have his weekly break of twenty-four hours. This was found to be necessary when there was no paid Warden available for relief. In the early days of the War, it was considered necessary for two full-time Wardens to be at the Post during the hours of darkness, but later on this ruling was relaxed and one 'staff man' was on duty alone.

The Post came to be the 'Enquire-within-upon-everything'. Though primarily the place to which incidents were reported for immediate transmission to the Report Centre, Police or Fire Control, a host of other information was stored. There was a card index system, consisting of one card for every house which came within the eight sections controlled from the Post, and shown thereon was the name of each member of the household. It was possible to ascertain from the cards the sizes of the gas masks issued, whether each had been fitted with a 'contex' and also if the holder had received ear plugs. Duplicate sets of these cards were in the possession of one Warden in each sector. A complete record of equipment issued to Wardens was available: civilian-duty respirator, anti-dim, steel helmet, overalls, battle-dress, great coats, beret, mackintosh, gum boots, ankle boots, electric lamp or torch, eye shield, first aid box, shelter key, whistle, rattle, bell and anti-gas clothing! Most of the latter (though a few were allocated to certain Wardens) were kept at the Post and hung round the room, suspended by hangers from the picture rail. All this equipment was obtained very gradually, stretching over a long period. In fact, boots were not issued until December 1941 and the first lot of battle-dress and great-coats were not received until January 1942.

It was towards the end of 1941 that the Wardens' Hardship Fund came into being, to which all Wardens were asked to contribute three pence each week. This fund was created to enable financial help to be given to any Warden who should suddenly find himself in difficult circumstances, either through becoming an air-raid casualty, or through any other reason.

Each week, lists were prepared for Headquarters, showing the number of hours that each voluntary Warden in each sector would be available in case of need. A further list was completed each week giving the number of hours that each Warden had actually been on duty, at least as far as actual 'Alerts' were concerned. Eventually, the 'powers that were' decided that these records need no longer be prepared. Divisional Orders, known as 'D.O.s' were for ever being received, and these were indexed and filed in numerical order. All this information was compiled by the permanent Wardens to whom a debt of gratitude is due in view of their never failing conscientiousness, reliability and courtesy. The Division Orders related to everything appertaining to the Wardens' Service: enemy aircraft, bombs, relief of the distressed, public shelters and the reporting of incidents, etc.

The most interesting article in the Post, however, was the Log Book, in which every incident reported at the Post was recorded, whether an actual raid or anything else that occurred in the area, and which affected the Wardens. For some unknown reason the Log Book was always treated with the utmost respect, and no facetious entry ever found its way into the pages.

At noon, on Sunday, the 18th January 1942, there came into being the standard types of Log Book and Register. The latter, at least, was received with no great enthusiasm or admiration, for it seemed to be a typical example of officialdom's idea of efficiency – sound in theory but cumbersome in practice. All Wardens, Police or any official visitor to the Post, from now on, were expected to sign on in the Register when entering and to sign off before leaving, after stating in the Register the duty performed or the reason for the visit. A column showing the period of duty performed, another showing the number of hours of duty previously performed during the lunar month, and still another column for the accumulative total of hours, had to be completed by all Wardens, who were expected to complete and sign the Register for all duties undertaken. There were two of these Registers and at the end of each week, one was collected for inspection, when the other came back into operation.

On Thursday, the 5th February 1942, there came into force, as an amendment to the Defence Regulations, an order whereby all part-time A.R.P. personnel were placed on the same footing as full-time members. By this order, termed the 'Freezing of part-time members', it was intended that all voluntary Wardens should perform at least 48 hours duty per lunar month, failing which they would be liable to the same penalties as full-time Wardens. As it is not desired to record in detail anything which may recall the many pin-pricks of officialdom with which the Wardens had to contend, it is not intended to dwell on this memory. Suffice to say that the fact that in the past Wardens had placed no limit whatever to their hours of service when necessary was apparently overlooked and forgotten.

However, the fears of the Wardens that duties would be 'manufactured' to keep them 'alive' were more or less dispersed. Whether the fact that the local press supported the agitation of the Wardens against any such treatment had any effect on the decision eventually arrived at is not known. It is enough to say that the new regulations, when issued, stated that henceforth, except in the case of 'Alerts', Wardens were expected to do duty for at least 12 hours each week. Of this period, 8 hours were to be a definite time of availability, when the Warden was not to be away from his sector. The remaining 4 hours were to be spent, if required, on Post activities, Patrols or attending Refresher Courses, etc. Thus the Wardens kept their status, that is to say, their chief duty remained – availability in case of Air Raids. A highly complicated and intricate system was introduced whereby a Warden, from a code designated to him, was able to ascertain from a master rota when and what his duties were during the next twelve months. It was obviously the work of a gentleman not lacking in intelligence, but certainly totally ignorant of the work of a Warden. However, orders were now orders, and consequently, after much criticism, the duties of the Warden remained as before but rotas, etc. were evolved round the standard now laid down. Henceforth, when a Warden was on 'Code Duty', he attended at the Post, and signed the Attendance Register, in order to show that he was available to fill his obligations under the new regulations. Had it been decided to scrap our existing arrangements for those now presented, the efficiency of the service would have deteriorated considerably, therefore instead of pouring the milk into the jug, the jug was wrapped around the milk. However, it was from about this time that the wonderful spirit, which up till then had always existed at E.24A began very slowly, but very surely, to pass away. Direct pressure will always stop the flow of blood!

At about twenty minutes to eleven on the night of Monday, the 13th April 1942, an incident occurred at the Post, which is worth recalling perhaps, although it had no connection with air raid precautions. Two Wardens on their way home from the Post were confronted by a young man who had just attempted to frustrate a robbery which he had witnessed at the nearby Church Road and Yew Tree Lane Post Office. The Wardens returned to the Post with the young man, who was immediately given permission to telephone the Police, and shortly afterwards a Sergeant of the force arrived. After questioning the informer they left the Post together. It was later learnt that the thieves had afterwards been discovered by a War Reserve policeman attempting, in an isolated spot, to open the safe which they had carried away in a lorry. When challenged, the thieves threatened the constable, who thereupon blew his whistle, and R.A.F. men of a nearby barrage balloon unit came running to his aid. The thieves then abandoned the safe, made off in the lorry, and as far as could be discovered, were never captured.

It was on the 5th May 1942, that the Post lost the services of Warden Bernard D. Sanders, who on that day met with a fatal cycle accident while on his way home from work. All those who knew him will ever remember his quiet but cheerful disposition, and his pleasing smile. The funeral took place the following Saturday at Perry Barr Crematorium and it was with deep regret that an obituary notice was entered in the Log Book.

During the week-ends of May 1942, many of the Wardens of E.24A paid a visit to the District Report Centre at Fox Hollies Park in Acocks Green. Here, in this edifice built underground, was explained the procedure adopted from the time an Incident was reported from the Post until such time as the Incident was closed. The method of recording the services available at any time during a raid, the system of filing all reports relating to incidents, and many other points were all explained by the officer in charge, to an interested audience.

It was at about this time that an attempt was made to inaugurate a social side to the Wardens' Service, and eventually, on Wednesday the 8th July 1942, the first game of cricket took place in the evening, in Yardley Park. On Saturday, 18th July, the first match was played; it was against Marlborough Cricket Club in Stoney Lane, when the Wardens' side put up quite a creditable display, though they were finally beaten.

Commencing on Friday, the 7th August 1942, many of the Wardens commenced a voluntary (and unofficial) course of musketry, etc. at the Headquarters of the 38th Battalion of the Warwickshire Home Guard. Here, at Lyndon House, Barrows Lane, on each Friday night for four weeks, the Wardens were taught, amongst other things, how to handle the 'U.S.A. – P. 17–300' and much satisfaction was obtained from the lessons, which were thoroughly enjoyed, and from which much knowledge was obtained. The course was concluded by each man firing on the miniature .22 Range. At the invitation of the 38th Battalion, the

Wardens attended a Drumhead Service on Sunday, the 6th September 1942, held in the grounds of Lyndon House.

It was in the October of 1942, that a large number of young ladies began to be 'directed' into the Wardens' Service. With every respect to the newcomers, it was generally felt at E.24A that this was neither in the best interests of the service, nor of the ladies themselves. However, it was now no longer possible to hope for the administrative side to be guided by the opinions of the ordinary Warden, and so the ladies came!

During this same month a 'First Aid Circle' was formed, and each Tuesday evening at the Post, a band of Wardens gathered together and became bandaged Wardens. From these informal meetings was gained much useful knowledge, and the gatherings were always a source of both interest and pleasure.

In order to save expense, and also to make the best use of the manpower of the country, the services of many of the full-time Wardens were dispensed with on the 7th November 1942. As a consequence, Post E.24A lost the full time services of Miss Osborne and Mr Taylor, both of whom had so very ably fulfilled their duties there since the commencement of the war as day and night Wardens respectively. Their departure met with great and genuine regret from every Warden attached to the Post, as well as from the two Wardens themselves. Thereafter the Post was manned by voluntary Wardens from 7 o'clock to 11 o'clock each evening, and at all other times was placed on 'Siren Call'. The latter expression, it will be recollected, meant that the Post was closed, except, of course, in the event of an 'Alert' when the manning again became the responsibility of the volunteers.

Sunday, the 15th November 1942 was selected as the first 'Civil Defence Sunday' and on the morning of that day, a large number of Wardens attended at the Warwick Cinema to see the films 'Invasion' and 'The Next of Kin'. During the afternoon, there was a divisional church parade, when the Methodist Church in Shirley Road, Acocks Green, was filled to overflowing.

Owing to its being required by the occupants of the house, the room which for so long had been E.24A was vacated at 11 o'clock on the night of Saturday, the 21st November 1942. Apparently, notice to quit had been served for some little time, but it was not until about 8 o'clock of the same evening any Warden attached to the Post knew of the position! Consequently, during the last three hours, there was a hectic rush to collect and store the paraphernalia accumulated since the first day of tenancy. Other duties had to be performed and Wardens were advised that when on code duty etc. they should attend at a nearby Post E.29B at

Church Road Schools, and there sign the Register, to which place it had been temporarily removed. Pending the finding of a new 'home', permission was obtained for the reopening of the Post during an 'Alert', and in any case, the 'strong point' was always available, though the telephone had been cut off!

As was proved in 1940, the Wardens' Service never let the Civil Defence side down, and consequently no great enthusiasm was ever shown for the monthly lectures, nor for the exercises and elimination contests that from time to time were now being 'thrust' upon the Wardens. Experience had proved that the Warden who excelled in theory was not by a long way bound to be the most efficient in time of raids. The apparent fear of those in authority that Wardens might lose their zest, was not shared by the Wardens themselves.

Eventually, Post E.24A was re-established, in what was previously a dressing room in the sports pavilion of the Co-operative Playing Fields situated in Barrows Lane. The fact that this room did not become available until Wednesday, the 6th January 1943, was not the fault of any Warden attached to the Post. For 46 days and nights, all had been perturbed at having no Post, and it was fortunate that during all this period there was not one 'Alert'. The new place was a great improvement on the previous one, especially in the fact that it was more or less self-contained. The telephone was eventually installed at the new Post, on Monday the 8th February 1943 – 79 days after the unexpected evacuation from Church Road! For this magnificent feat of rapidity of movement no credit was due to any Warden attached to the Post. The wireless set, long since given to the Post, was re-installed in the new surroundings and eventually both an electric fire and ring were fixed by the authorities. With the loaning 'for the duration' (by generous Wardens) of a chest of drawers and a clock, the Post became almost furnished.

The history of E.24A would not be complete if no mention was made of the many Wardens directed into the service late in 1942 or in 1943. Some time elapsed before their training was completed and before all were fully equipped – and incidentally much work was caused thereby to many others. All Wardens were now exempt from fire watching, and consequently many volunteers were re-directed into the service to adjust an anomaly whereby volunteers had been compelled to fire watch, whilst the directed Wardens were exempt. This, involving as it did the issuing and completing of forms, caused much 'running around', as did the manning of the Post each evening from 7 p.m. to 11 p.m. This latter, and ever present, task was not always easy, many Wardens not being available through various reasons, and thus the Wardens' Service was not allowed to rust! A 'strong point' for the new Post was commenced in August 1943 and at the same time the one at the old Post was demolished. It was hoped that the new one would be utilised as much as the old – for it had never once been occupied for the purpose for which it was erected! A course on Artificial Respiration – practice and theory – under the auspices of the Royal Life Saving Society was commenced on Wednesday, the 8th September 1943, at Starbank Road Schools. On the floor of a hall in this school, quite a few Wardens from E.24A rolled and turned each other over, and after a few weeks' tuition, after successfully passing the test, were awarded a badge with which to decorate their uniforms, together with a certificate.

In March 1944 the great majority of the Wardens who had been 'directed' to E.24A, were transferred to other Posts, not 'blessed' with many Wardens. Thus, the strength of E.24A was brought back, approximately, to that prevailing in 1940. It was at about this time, that a team of three Wardens from the Post, representing Group E.24, distinguished themselves by reaching the final of the Division in the Annual Quiz competition for the city, the grand final of which was staged on the 13th May 1944.

A questionnaire was received at the Post, in May 1944, on the subject of a post-war Civil Defence Wardens' Service. Each Warden was asked to state his views, and the only conclusion drawn from the replies was that all the Wardens wished to retain after the cessation of hostilities were the friendships formed. It was not thought necessary for any special organization to be formed for this ambition to be realised.

In common with the other Defence Services, one red chevron for each complete year of wartime service was issued to the members of the Wardens' Service in July 1944 – 'to be worn on the right sleeve, 3½ inches from the end.'

As a perpetual memory of the Wardens' Service in Birmingham, the 'powers that were' asked that there should be endowed a number of hospital beds in the City Hospitals. Each group was requested to raise a certain sum, and the target for Group E.24 was fixed at £80. By means of socials, whist drives, one dance, and individual and other efforts (including a dart-board for the first time at Post E.24A!) the splendid sum of £173:4:7 was raised by the end of September 1944.

Owing to the virtual disappearance of the Luftwaffe, and the victorious advance of the Allied armies on the continent, the Government deemed it safe for black-out regulations to be considerably relaxed as from the 17th September 1944. The Home Guard were told to 'Stand Easy' and Fire

Guard duties were suspended. However, the Wardens' Service carried on – in more ways than one – its duties slightly relieved, but not to the extent that the Wardens themselves considered possible and reasonable.

Notwithstanding the fact that Civil Defence was on its last legs, between 20 and 30 Wardens of Group E.24 were still enthusiastic enough to attend a series of lectures on First Aid. The classes, each lasting about 2 hours, were held at Hob Moor Road School on Tuesday evenings at 8 o'clock, for about eight consecutive weeks, commencing 26th September 1944. Each entrant succeeded in securing a certificate, as a result of an examination held on the 19th December.

It was fully expected by many, that heavy raids from enemy aircraft would be experienced if, and when, our armies invaded the continent. However, happily for us, such fears did not materialise, and Birmingham was fortunate in being just outside the range of V.1's ad V.2's.

On the 12th October 1944, the Wardens' Service was decoded, and E.24A was manned by volunteers, and only between the hours of 8 p.m. and 10 p.m. In order that they should not forget one another(!), a photograph of the Wardens of Group E.24 was taken on the Co-operative Sports Ground during the morning of Sunday, the 29th October 1944.

Post E.24A was finally relinquished on the 16th January 1945, and the Wardens were asked to attend, henceforth, at Post E.24B. Some there were who duly fulfilled this request, but there were others who were not so enthusiastic.

All 'Black-out' regulations were finally withdrawn on the 23rd April 1945, and the Civil Defence organization officially ceased to exist on the 2nd May 1945.

War in Europe came to an end in May, and a final parade was arranged for Sunday, the 3rd June 1945. Unfortunately, the weather was wretched, and consequently the number of wardens who paraded was very small – and thus E.24A faded out of existence, undoubtedly for ever.

As time went on, and more and more Wardens came into the ring, including many ladies, it was positively amazing to find that the original bon-homie remained, entirely unspoilt. With over 130 Wardens attached to the Post, it was natural that all types, ages, creeds, occupations and political faiths should be represented, yet never once can it be recollected that any dissension arose. The only reason for this truly remarkable and astounding record seemed to be attributable to the fact that each one had the same desire – to help his, or her, fellow citizens, and to aid in easing their lot in the senseless hell let loose. However, one finds it hard to believe that the same spirit could possibly have prevailed at every Wardens' Post, and so it must be left as a fact, for which one must be truly grateful.

Siren Memories

It was half past eleven on the night of the 25th June 1940 that the inhabitants of our city were first disturbed by the wailing of the sirens, indicating that a visit from enemy aircraft was a possibility. Fortunately, the possibility did not become a reality and after 53 minutes the sirens were again heard, but this time in one continuous even note, indicating the 'Raiders Passed' signal. Forty five Wardens were on duty during this first period of 'Alertness' and afterwards signed off at Post E.24A in the Log Book, where many strange and interesting entries had been and were yet to be recorded.

Before the end of the following August, the sirens had wailed their warnings on nearly thirty occasions, but instead of giving confidence to the public, they had had rather a disturbing effect. On occasions, bombs were heard falling in the distance before the warning had been issued, and the 'Raiders Passed' had been sounded whilst enemy aircraft could be heard overhead and while gunfire was still in progress. The 'Raiders Passed' signal had been followed within a few minutes by another 'Warning' and consequently the public had been making hurried exits from beds to shelters, shelters to beds, then again beds to shelters. This ordeal was far worse, of course, for those with the responsibility of small children, and old people. So lacking was confidence in the sirens, and not without justification, that Vigilance Patrols were organized by, or with the aid of, Wardens. Members of the public undertook, in turns, to patrol the roads at night and upon observing searchlights, hearing aircraft, gun fire or bombs, they roused their neighbours by various means. In some roads, each house was fitted with a bell, and a master push was utilised when the warning was required to be given. Others contented themselves with shouting, 'Enemy Aircraft!' and by the knocking of front doors, or the banging of dust-bin lids. Hopeless confusion was caused on several nights, and on one occasion, complaints were received at the Post that the sounding of bells had been heard in the district, the noise of which was intended to be applicable to the signal 'All Clear' after a gas attack. After much investigation it was discovered that, in one sector, the Vigilance Patrol, believing they had cause to give warning, had banged stench-pipes with iron bars, with most effective and reverberating effect. To find the culprits was not easy, and to persuade them of the error of their ways was a still harder task. As a few nights previously incendiary bombs had been dropped in the district in question, it was with sympathy that the Wardens approached those who had erred, both in the method of their warning and also in the fact of giving the warning at all, there being no enemy activity present!

In another sector, the Vigilance Patrol one early morning were a little too vigilant, and awoke all their neighbours, who promptly took to their shelters. When the Wardens, after various enquiries, were satisfied that a mistake had been made, the Vigilance Patrol were advised that as it was a case of mistaken enthusiasm, those who had aroused their neighbours from their beds should see that they were returned.

Fortunately for all concerned, it was considered safe after a few weeks to place more trust in the sirens, and the Vigilance Patrols faded away into obscurity, to the general relief of all concerned, including the Wardens.

During one raid, when heavy gun fire had been experienced, and the seemingly endless 'chug-chug-chug' of Jerry planes overhead had become an unpleasant monotony, those at the Post were suddenly roused from their air of weariness to one of expectancy. The telephone bell rang, and the voice at the other end was that of one of the Wardens asking for an opinion. An unpleasant odour was pervading his area, resembling the smell of burning wood, or of garden refuse. The Warden was anxious to know if the odour could be detected from the Post and sure enough, upon investigation outside, there was indeed an unusual smell. Strange to relate, although it was thought that possibly the enemy might have resorted to the use of gas, no-one seemed unduly alarmed, though gas masks were extracted, and cleaned in readiness. The Warden, over the telephone, was advised to await developments and not to utilise his rattle. It was then that someone remembered hearing rumours about a smoke-screen, of which however, no official intimation had been received. It was rightly conjectured that the cause of the alarm was indeed the smoke screen, but the rattles came very close to being used that night, on the principle of 'better safe than sorry'. In cold print this little episode may not sound very disturbing, but in actuality it was rather unsettling, for no one was very anxious to make the decision as to whether the gas alarm should be given or not. So much for the first experience of the smoke screen around the E.24A area.

Some weeks after this event, during another raid, two Wardens reported that the pavements were covered with spots of oil or grease, each about the size of half-a-crown. Liquid gas, sprayed from above, was the possibility felt, though not really thought to be a probability. However, it was the Warden's task to take every reasonable precaution, and to make every investigation into things unusual, and so a decision 'on the spots' had to be made 'on the spot'. Consequently, five or six Wardens went out to examine the pavement and had no difficulty in observing the causes of concern, and, one by one, each placed his nose to a spot, and inhaled through the nostrils. One of the party then made the remark that if gas it was, none of their number would be alive to tell the tale! Fortunately, there was no fulfillment of this suggestion, and it was finally agreed that the spots had been caused by warm rain passing through the prevailing smoke-screen, setting up condensation and thereby causing the oil to descend to the earth in liquid form. It was further agreed that to an unsuspecting public, it might have had a most disturbing effect.

The telephone at the Post often caused trouble, but just after the commencement of one raid, it failed completely, as did all the telephones on the same exchange. Arrangements were hurriedly made for the alternative method of transmitting messages in case of need. Wardens with cycles were hastily summoned and eventually it was discovered that at a Post not very far away (but on a different exchange) the telephone was still in order. Fortunately, no incident or message was that night received and therefore it was not necessary to call upon the cyclists. Strange to relate, the telephone at E.24A was found to be operating as soon as the 'Raiders Passed' signal sounded.

Vague reports were more than once received during raids, of unexploded bombs having been heard to fall 'somewhere between "A" and "B", or perhaps more towards "C" and behind "B" '. Though not sure of the scene of the incident the bearer of the report, whether Warden or civilian, was generally confident that the bomb had been heard to drop, but that no explosion had occurred. It must be borne in mind, that no such report could be ignored, and required investigation. After much searching in one such case, the Warden who was looking suddenly came across what he thought to be the small aperture denoting the place of entry of a bomb which had failed to explode, or the action of which was possibly delayed. It was in a garden at the rear of a row of cottages, the raid was still in progress, and the householders were in their shelters. Excitedly, he yelled to the policemen who was also searching, 'Here it is! I've found it!' Then a voice from a shelter shouted back, 'That's a hole I dug yesterday to get some soil to cover the shelter!' Sure enough, there was a number of similar excavations in the garden.

During a particularly heavy raid, so many reports had been received of suspected delayed action bombs in a particular location, that in the early hours of the morning, when it was just getting light, after the 'Raiders Passed' had been sounded, a small party of Wardens set out to make an extensive and thorough search. The scene was a Municipal Sports Ground in Queens Road, in which was a barrage balloon and crew, and consequently, entrance was in itself a difficulty. Failing to make themselves heard, the party moved cautiously across the field, until a figure could be seen in the morning mist, complete with rifle and bayonet, and a challenge rang out, 'Halt! Who goes there?' The answer given was, 'Friends – A.R.P. Wardens' and they were allowed to advance and make their mission known. Eventually, the officer in charge gave full permission for the field to be searched and agreed that so much 'blue pencil' stuff had fallen around him that night, that no amazement would be expressed by him, if any unexploded bomb was close to hand. The field was duly combed without success, but the experience had not been lacking in excitement.

There was one particular sector which within quite a short period had had more than its quota of serious incidents and perhaps for that reason, anything unusual was seized upon as something dangerous. A sound resembling the ticking of a clock had been heard proceeding from a house which had been vacated by its owners, owing to its proximity to a bomb which had failed to explode and which was receiving the attention of the Bomb Disposal Squad. The complaint was received more than once, but each time a Warden investigated, he was unlucky and could hear no sound. Eventually, the police were summoned and finally discovered that in the unoccupied house, water was running from the bathroom and dripping on to the glass roof of a verandah below.

One night, during an 'Alert' period, when no bombs had been heard to fall, but planes had been heard passing over in one monotonous drone, a message was received over the telephone at the Post. It came from a house in Stoney Lane, in the adjoining sub-division, and a lady's voice asked if someone would visit her as she feared an object of destruction had descended in her garden. Unfortunately, no Warden was available at the Post, but the lady was informed that the Wardens' Post nearest to her home would be notified immediately, and the promise was kept. However shortly afterwards, the 'Raiders Passed' was sounded and two Wardens immediately set out to visit the house in question, in case no one had been able to investigate.

The house was found to be quite a large detached one, and the entrance was heavily sandbagged. The Wardens were welcomed and invited inside, but were told that the police had been already and discovered that the moonlight had cast an ugly looking shadow across the garden, which from a distance, to anxious eyes, might well have appeared to be an object dropped from the skies. It had been first observed after a bout of heavy gun fire, which further increased suspicion. As the windows at the back of the house had been already blown out by the blast from a bomb in a previous raid, cause for nervousness was excusable. However, it was more than that, it was very easily understood, when it was learnt that the only occupants of the house were a gallant old lady of 95 and her daughter! These two, though living in a lovely home, were reduced to spending each night on the floor of the hall, but they obstinately refused to move into an area considered to be more secure. Such was life in the autumn of 1940.

During many raids there were numerous reports received by, or from, Wardens of lighting offences, damage by shrapnel, breakage of telephone wires, the drifting of barrage balloons and unexploded bombs. All these reports, of course, required attention and some necessitated notification to the police or Report Centre. Happily, in the case of unexploded bombs, the reports were in the great majority of cases found to be mistaken.

When the sirens sounded the 'Warning' (afterwards changed to the 'Alert') the Wardens immediately were on duty and so remained until the 'Raiders Passed' signal. They then journeyed to the Post, where they often stayed for quite a while until the 'All Clear' or 'White' was received over the telephone from the Head Warden of the Sub-Division, signifying that they could return to their homes. The Wardens then signed off duty in the Log Book, but in early raids almost as often as not, another 'Warning' would be heard before long. It was during this period that if, after the 'Raiders Passed' had been sounded, a certain Warden attended the Post, enemy activity seemed to re-open automatically. The 'spell' became so real, that if there had been no incidents, the Warden eventually refrained from coming to the Post, but asked his colleagues to sign him off duty!

Eventually, the 'All Clear' was abolished, and Wardens signed off after the sounding of 'Raiders Passed', which met with the general approval of all concerned!

Raid Memories

Although on 13th August 1940, a stick of high explosive bombs had been dropped on Yardley Park and Almshouse within one hundred yards or so of one of the E.24A sectors, it was in the early hours of 16th August 1940, that the Post sent out its first Action Report. The voluntary Warden, whose duty was the responsibility of the Post, made his way there as soon as the sirens sounded. However, so immediate was enemy activity that before he reached his destination, he saw at about one hundred yards beyond the Post, the blackness of the night broken by a dazzling brilliance. Even as he continued on his way, ghostly figures appeared out of the darkness and, silhouetted against the glaring background, were observed to be successfully tackling the incendiary bomb. Hardly had the Warden entered the Post, before a colleague off a nearby sector raced in, saying that immediate help was required from the Fire Service, as many incendiary bombs had been dropped in the area, causing fires to be started in several houses, but that there were no known casualties. Over the telephone the Fire Control was contacted and the Report Centre notified. Thus the first Action Report from Post E.24A was sent, almost before the sound of the last siren had faded away.

Altogether, that night, quite a few Action Reports were made and hundreds of incendiary bombs were dropped in six different roads – Stoney Lane, Heathmere Avenue, Charminster Avenue, Rockingham Road, Wroxton Road, Church Road – causing many fires, most of which were extinguished by the Wardens before any great damage could materialise. However, at least six houses were badly burned, and three or four garages sustained damage, but fortunately there were no casualties. The Wardens had had their baptism, but so had the incendiaries.

On the 24th August 1940, at least six high explosive bombs were dropped, within a hundred yards of one of the sectors, but fortunately descended in the Municipal Sports Ground, causing no damage. On the night of the 26th/27th August 1940, two houses in Patrick Road, in the E.24A area suffered slight damage to ceilings through the blast from bombs dropped in an adjacent district.

The next time the enemy caused material destruction on the E.24A area was 3rd September 1940. One heavy bomb descended off Church Road quite close to the post, but fortunately buried itself in a tennis court. A delayed action bomb was found in a garden of a house in Croft Road, from which the residents were hastily evacuated. The bomb

Lydsard Grove August 14th 1940

Nurses' Home, Yardley Green Sanatorium August 23rd 1940

Rosedale Grove off Hobmoor Road, Yardley September 5th 1940

Shelter of Home in Rowland Road, Yardley September 5th 1940

exploded a few hours later causing only slight damage to property, and there were no casualties.

In the adjoining road, Patrick Road, a further unexploded bomb was found and the residents were removed. This bomb duly received the attention of the military authorities, but offered serious resistance to extraction. On the evening of the 18th September, fifteen days after being dropped – and when the Bomb Disposal Squad had gone off duty until the next day – the bomb exploded. About six houses were made absolutely uninhabitable, whilst many others suffered considerably and the windows of scores were shattered. As four days was considered to be the longest period for the action of a bomb to be delayed, it was concluded that the bomb was a dud, which had been set in motion by the attempt at removal.

Although almost every night during the next few weeks the sirens wailed their warnings, and often some part of the city suffered through the Luftwaffe, it was not until the night of the 22nd October 1940, that E.24A found itself again in the front line. Two Wardens were standing outside the Post watching the terrific barrage when suddenly there was a noise as of an express train, seemingly coming in their direction. As no railway was near by, the Wardens thought it best to flatten themselves. It was indeed no locomotive but nevertheless a train – of incendiaries – which fell all around, lighting up the surrounding district with a startling vividness. Numerous incendiary bombs descended in open spaces – including the garden at the Post – and in nine different roads: Homecroft Road, Croft Road, Stoney Lane, Vera Road, Church Road, Wroxton Road, Heathmere Avenue, Charminster Avenue and Patrick Road, causing more or less slight damage in many houses before being extinguished.

One of the incendiary bombs which penetrated the roof of a house was tackled by one Warden standing in the bath (already filled with water) and operating a stirrup pump from there, whilst a colleague forced himself through the small aperture leading to the loft and succeeded in extinguishing the fire. Strange to relate, when that same Warden went next day to view the result of his labours, he found, much to his astonishment, that try as he would, he could not persuade his body to pass through that aperture again!

Two high explosive bombs demolished or rendered absolutely useless four houses in two different roads, Patrick Road and Vera Road, and the adjoining houses were seriously affected. Luck was again with E.24A, in that there were no casualties. On this night a delayed action bomb fell in Moat Lane, just off the E.24A area, close to a garage, and during the next raid, on the 25th/26th October 1940, it exploded, damaging the gas mains and causing a fire. From Post E.24A, the Fire Control was contacted, and afterwards the Report Centre notified. This fire was extinguished with difficulty, and it was with relief that the glow in the sky was seen from the Post eventually to disappear.

The sirens sounded the 'Raiders Passed' as early as 11.38 p.m. on the 8th November 1940, and after the 'All Clear' had been received, the Wardens returned to their homes to 'Stand by'. On their way from the Post, a party of five or six Wardens, at about twenty minutes past midnight, suddenly heard the noise of an approaching aeroplane, which appeared to be in difficulties. Whistles were blown as the aircraft flew directly over their heads at an extremely low altitude, and almost immediately the plane dropped what appeared to be incendiary bombs in the adjacent Yardley Park. The 'incendiaries' appeared to burn out immediately, and as the Wardens with difficulty made their way into the park, a terrific crash was heard. No trace of the bombs could be found, but the smell of magnesium was strong round the old moat, into which it was presumed they had fallen. After further investigation it was learnt that the plane had crashed about a mile away, on the railway lines at Stechford, and all the occupants had been killed. It was, however, with the deepest regret, that later on in the day the Wardens were led to believe that the plane was a British bomber, and that the 'incendiaries' were, in reality, signals of distress.

During the night of the 14th – 15th November 1940, German bombers brought devastation to the city of Coventry – the first real 'blitz' on a British town. The sirens sounded the 'Warning' in our city that night at 7.5 p.m. and the 'Raiders Passed' was not heard until 11 hours and 11 minutes later – at 6.16 a.m. The glow from the fires caused at Coventry was plainly discernible from our side of the city and the enemy's aircraft were heard practically without ceasing throughout the night. One particularly heavy bomb – originally intended for Coventry, apparently – caused severe damage and casualties not a mile from Post E.24A at Lily Road. Twelve persons were killed alone from this one bomb.

Warnings continued to be nightly affairs, Birmingham a constant target, and heavy gun fire a common occurrence. Wardens never failed to report, however many times the sirens moaned their warning. Eventually our city was well and truly 'blitzed' and much damage and many casualties were inflicted during the 9½ hours that the raid lasted. Bombs of all calibre were dropped round the E.24A area, on that terrible night of the 19th – 20th November 1940. From the Post itself, three Action

Vera Road, Yardley November 23rd 1940

Vera Road, Yardley November 23rd 1940

Lily Road, Yardley November 14th 1940

Lily Road, Yardley (General view) November 14th 1940

Lily Road, Yardley November 14th 1940

Reports were transmitted to the Report Centre. A high explosive bomb was dropped in Blakesley Road in the area, wrecking four houses, and causing damage of various degrees to about thirty or forty more houses. Blakesley Hall itself was damaged. Fortunately, there were only two casualties, one person suffering from shock and one from only superficial injuries. Although only the chimney stack of his home remained, the chief concern of one man was that he had lost his ferrets and feared they would destroy his fowl!

Incendiary bombs fell in another sector in Farnol Road, Vibart Road, Barrows Lane and the playing field, and about twenty fires were extinguished by Wardens before any damage to property was caused. In Vera Road, in another sector, incendiaries fell and one dropped in a garage adjoining a house, causing damage to a motor-cycle and side-car. The owner was burnt and taken to hospital, and the fire was eventually extinguished by Wardens. The following night, the 20th–21st November 1940, three parachutes were observed from Vibart Road to be falling in a certain direction, and the Report Centre was duly notified.

Only two nights after, on the 22nd–23rd November 1940, there was another severe blitz on our city, lasting about 11 hours. That night there was more activity at Post E.24A than ever before, so numerous and – what then appeared – catastrophic, were the incidents.

Quite early in the evening, at 7.37 p.m., a Warden reported that two high explosive bombs and an oil bomb had dropped in his area of Rockingham Road and Charminster Avenue, and that three persons had been killed, whilst five people had received superficial injuries. One of the three killed was an unfortunate young woman who had been bombed out of her own home only a few days previously, and had sought refuge with friends. One road, Charminster Avenue, was partly obstructed by the oil bomb, which burst, but fortunately failed to ignite, and lay in the roadway. Three houses were totally wrecked and numerous other houses were severely or slightly damaged. An Incident Post was established in the home of a Warden. Later in the night, in the same area, a delayed action bomb was traced by police and Wardens, in a garage. The people in the vicinity were immediately moved to a place of safety in Church Road School, and the bomb exploded at about 9 o'clock the following morning, completely demolishing two houses, and wrecking another.

Incendiaries fell in the playground of the nearby Church Road School, close to a First Aid Post, and the Fire Service was summoned. Across the road, a high explosive bomb damaged another school, Hobmoor Road. These last two incidents were both reported through Post E.24A, though actually the scenes of damage were both just outside its area. The reason for this was that a little time previous, a woman had been brought to the Post, suffering from injuries to the hand, caused through blast; First Aid was rendered and the casualty was escorted to the First Aid Post by the Warden, who reported these two incidents.

In another sector, Patrick Road, a high explosive bomb caused very serious damage to two houses and damaged six others, whilst two in Vera Road suffered slightly. In the same area of Vera Road, an incendiary bomb started a fire in a bedroom, but was extinguished by Wardens. The body of a man was found in Church Road, killed through a high explosive bomb, which otherwise did little damage. In still another spot in Church Road, a house was set on fire by an oil bomb, and was absolutely and completely burnt out. One man was severely burned, and was taken to the First Aid Post for treatment, but eventually died of his injuries. The tragedy of this fire was that the Fire Service was summoned and attended, but no water was available as a result of the raid of the 19th – 20th November.

It was during this raid that the gun encampment adjoining the E.24A area received special attention from the enemy, and the bravery of a bombardier at the camp was afterwards recognized by the award of the

Back of Steyning Road, Yardley *Raid 64*

Station Road, Yardley *May 13th 1941*

Stoney Lane, Yardley May 13th 1941

Highfield Road, May 18th 1941

Military Medal. No one residing in our city during the night of 22nd – 23rd November 1940 will need much reminding of its awfulness. The majority of the Wardens were by now returning home from work each evening, to snatch a quick tea and immediately after to don their overalls pending the Warning signal. If time was still available, an attempt was then made to catch a few moments' sleep before being roused by the sirens, or maybe by unwelcome guests circling overhead. As he well knew, the Warden would have little chance to really rest again until the coming dawn, which invariably seemed to be the only influence to cause the Raiders to depart. It was seldom that a Warden saw anyone during a raid other than his colleagues except members of the Police Force and others engaged on official civil defence duties.

The next time that any damage was caused on the E.24A area, through enemy action, was when a high explosive bomb dropped just outside the Post area, at ten minutes before midnight on the 11th December 1940. This incident was reported from the adjacent Post, and a row of shops in the Yew Tree area suffered very considerable damage, and some were made untenable. Many houses and shops in Church Road and Stoney Lane suffered broken windows, damage to tiles and roofs, etc. through the blast from this bomb. This raid will be remembered if only for the fact that it was Birmingham's longest 'blitz', the attack lasting for 13 hours and 9 minutes, with the exception of two short breaks of 13 and 39 minutes respectively. During the 122 days of September, October, November and December in 1940 the number of 'Alerts' had been no less than 217 by both day and night, and the total number of hours involved 415 (Sept. 50 – 80 hrs, Oct. 70 – 125 hrs, Nov. 62 – 128 hrs, Dec. 35 – 82 hrs.)

By January 1941, warnings had gradually become a little less frequent, presumably through the weather conditions not being so suitable for night flying. However, on the night of 9th – 10th April 1941 there was an extremely heavy raid on Birmingham and the enemy let loose on the E.24A area five high explosive bombs. Fortunately again, there were no casualties, but there was one remarkable escape when a large house at the corner of Church Road and Queens Road was demolished. Another of the bombs wrecked an air-raid shelter, the owners of which, by providence, were not inside. The blast from this bomb smashed many windows in the vicinity. In the same road, a further high explosive bomb dropped in the roadway, bursting both the gas and the water mains, whilst in Vibart Road the water main was fractured by another bomb. The last of these five bombs caused no damage, falling in open ground by the side of a cottage in Blakesley Road. It was on this night that about four to six bombs fell in the grounds of the Yardley Vicarage, yet only the kitchen and outhouses were damaged. During this raid, First Aid was rendered at the Post to a member of the Home Guard, who had received superficial injuries to the hand. Two Wardens also received treatment for slight injuries caused through falls. The next night, there was yet another heavy raid on the side of the city in which was Post E.24A, but by good fortune no incident had to be reported from that Post.

Siren 'Alerts', as they had now been termed for some time, became still less frequent, but in the very early hours of 17th May 1941, a shower of incendiaries fell near the Post and the surrounding district. The Fire Service could not be contacted direct over the telephone, but were summoned via the Report Centre. These incendiaries were of both the explosive and the non-explosive types, and at least eight different roads were affected: Church Road, Croft Road, Homecroft Road, Vera Road, Vibart Road, Stoney Lane, Barrows Lane and Heathmere Avenue. At least eight houses suffered more or less slight damage, chiefly in bedrooms, and two garden sheds were burnt. In most cases however, the bombs were extinguished by Wardens and members of the Fire Parties before any serious fires were started.

During the next few months there was a definite pause in enemy activity over Britain, and it was very seldom that the siren warnings were sounded. In fact, after the raid of the 17th May 1941, the sirens were heard only on two more occasions during May, eight in June, three in July, two in August – and during September there was not a single period of Alertness. Nevertheless, during the early days of October, a 'strong point' was erected alongside the Post. This was built in the front garden of the house, the front room of which constituted Post E.24A. The strongpoint was a brick-built edifice, with concrete top, about 6 feet long, 4 feet wide, and 6½ feet high. It was intended for occupation during heavy raids, and of course a telephone extension from the Post was eventually installed (in September 1942!), but space was very limited. During its construction, one wondered if it was always true that coming events cast their shadows before them!

'Alerts' continued to be very spasmodic affairs, and it was seldom indeed that any enemy activity was heard. However, at a quarter past one, on the morning of Sunday, the 11th January 1942, satisfaction was obtained from the sight of a German bomber falling in flames to the east of Birmingham.

Notwithstanding the absence of air raids, the keeness of the enthusiastic Wardens in no way abated. Light patrols, of course, continued, as also did the manning of the Post, on occasional weekends.

During heavy falls of snow, Wardens were expected to see that all fire hydrants were kept clear and that salt (obtainable from the Post) was used to prevent freezing. In addition, there were periodic meetings at the Post and elsewhere, of the Wardens of the various sectors; all these duties helped interest to be maintained in the service that was now thankful to be only 'Standing by.'

The Police were notified on Saturday the 16th May 1942, that the attention of a Warden had been drawn to an unnatural looking cavity at the rear of a house in Rockingham Road. As this particular area had suffered rather considerably during the night of the 22nd–23rd November 1940, it was feared that possibly an unexploded bomb lay buried at this spot. The Warden was not satisfied, neither were the Police and so the military authorities were summoned. After investigations, the Bomb Disposal Squad finally decided that the suspicious looking hole had been dug by the previous occupants of the house. To those living in the immediate neighbourhood this came as quite a relief, for it was just at this time that an undiscovered bomb in London had exploded, causing much damage and some fatal casualties.

It was at about the same time, that in another sector, an over-anxious member of the community evacuated his neighbours because he suspected an unexploded bomb in his garden, owing to a crack in the ground and the sound of ticking. He called the local Warden, who assured him his suspicions were unfounded, as there would be a big hole, for only a heavy bomb would give forth a ticking noise. However, pacification was not obtained until the Police were summoned, when the conclusion arrived at was that the crack was caused by the dryness of the ground, and the noise was from a ticking spider in the vicinity!

After a long spell of inactivity, enemy aircraft caused the 'Alert' to be sounded six times in the last nine days of July 1942. In early daylight on Monday, the 27th July, bombs were dropped on Solihull, the first to be heard from Yardley for a long time, and in the very early hours of the following day, Tuesday, 28th July, there was a short but sharp attack on our city. That early morning, there were once again, all the old and familiar, but unpleasant, sights and noises, and in addition there were seen and heard in action for the first time, the rocket guns. The drone of heavy bombers, the rat-tat-tat of machine guns, the pattern of tracer bullets, the sound of falling shrapnel, the thud of bombs and the booming of guns all brought back memories of the Autumn of 1940. At the sister Post – E.24B – it was reported that a missile about three feet long and about three to four inches in diameter had penetrated the roof of a Hobmoor Croft house and after various diversions, had finally come to rest in the foundations of the pantry. People in the close proximity were evacuated as a safeguard but afterwards it was considered safe for them to return to their homes, the missile being thought to be the casing of a flare or of a rocket gun shell, or part of the tail of a plane.

During the early hours of the following Thursday and Friday, 30th and 31st July, there were two more sharp raids on the West Midlands Area. Happily, the only incident to be reported from Post E.24A on 30th July was in respect of a crater about four feet in diameter and two feet deep that had been formed in the rear of a Heathmere Avenue house through a shell fired from a rocket gun. In the Friday morning raid, at 2 o'clock, there were dropped on the E.24A area very many incendiary bombs of a new and more dangerous type. The powers of penetration were terrific, and in all there were 21 incidents reported from the Post to the Report Centre. These bombs were dropped in nine different areas: Blakemere Avenue, Church Road, Croft Road, Heathmere Avenue, Hobmoor Road School, Homecroft Road, Rockingham Road, Stoney Lane and Wroxton Road. Unfortunately, a man was killed in Stoney Lane, and in the house next door, one of the Wardens received very nasty injuries whilst tackling a bomb in his own home, which suffered considerably. Another of the bombs penetrated through a well covered 'Anderson' shelter in Church Road, but fortunately the two lady occupants were able to make their exit before the explosion took place. Two more bombs penetrated a sufficient depth to fracture gas mains in Church Road and Heathmere Avenue, and another to damage a water main in Stoney Lane, where a fire was being tackled by the Fire Service. Fortunately, there were handy many receptacles already filled with water in case of such emergency, and under the directions of Wardens, a chain of buckets was quickly formed, with excellent results. Other bombs caused fires but comparatively slight damage, and many failed to explode, when the necessary precautions were taken to see that the public were warned to keep a safe distance, as delayed action was feared to be a possibility. Another bomb burst in a Homecroft Road front garden, and shot into the bedroom above, causing a fire to be started with subsequent damage to the room and contents. At least four bombs actually penetrated into the neighbouring Post – E.24B – and damage was caused before the fires were extinguished. One Warden was taken to the First Aid Post, and afterwards removed to Selly Oak Hospital where he was detained. For the remainder of the raid, 'business' had to be transacted from the home of the Assistant Chief Warden nearby. A man in the area of E.24B lost his life through a bomb exploding just as he was about to attempt its removal with his foot. The Regional Commissioner, Lord Dudley, visited Post E.24B during the evening of Thursday, the 3rd September, 1942. It was during this raid that a Warden was called into a house where there was an unexploded incendiary bomb, and close by, there lay a dark green object which the Warden suspected to be the explosive portion. Bravely, in the darkness, he picked it up and to his horror, he felt it move. He was preparing himself for the worse, when the lady of the house said 'No, Warden, that's my little boy's toy cannon!'

Although, of course, it was not then known, the raid of 31st July 1942, proved to be the last in which the enemy inflicted damage in the E.24A area. Indeed, it was only on 18 more occasions that the sirens were heard to wail the "Alert", and the "Raiders Passed" was last sounded at 1.50 a.m. on the morning of the 4th of March 1945.

Closing Memories

Out of most evil, there emerges some good. Through the creation of Post E.24A, many friendships were formed which were to last a lifetime, and the man who is rich in friends is never really poor.

When, in more ways than one, the days were dark, comradeships were made which proved to be like good wine – they improved with the passing of time.

Long before the cessation of hostilities, some consolation was obtained from the thought that, in all probability, the great majority of Nazi airmen who prowled over our heads in 1940 were no longer able to take any active interest in flying!

Very pleasant memories remain – even of the Autumn of 1940 – yet may it never be the lot of another generation to be welded together in friendship, through such a cause!

Statistics of Post E.24A

(Of these 373 "Alerts", 77 were officially recorded as "Raids")

No.	Date			Warning (or Alert)	Raiders Passed	Duration Hrs. Mins.
1	25/6	June	1940	11.30 pm	12.23 am	0–53
2	29/30	June		11.32 pm	1.45 am	2–13
3	6	July		10.10 pm	10.46 pm	0–36
4	22	July		12.08 am	12.15 pm	0–7
5	9	August		2.05 am	2.34 am	0–29
6	13/14	August		11.20 pm	12.10 am	0–50
7	14	August		12.11 am	12.12 am	0–1
8	14	August		12.14 am	3.07 am	2–53
9	16	August		1.40 am	3.17 am	1–37
10	17/18	August		11.50 am	3.00 am	3–10
11	18/19	August		10.45 pm	12.15 am	1–30
12	20	August		3.40 am	4.25 am	0–45
13	24	August		2.37 am	3.47 am	1–10
14	24	August		3.54 am	5.02 am	1–8
15	24	August		10.10 pm	11.47 pm	1–37
16	25	August		12.06 am	3.55 am	3–49
17	25	August		4.37 am	4.55 am	0–18
18	25/26	August		9.45 pm	3.50 am	6–5
19	25/26	August		4.02 am	4.48 am	0–46
20	26/27	August		9.50 pm	4.14 am	6–24
21	27	August		1.42 pm	1.48 pm	0–6
22	27/28	August		10.19 pm	2.43 am	4–24
23	28	August		3.00 am	3.16 am	0–16
24	28	August		3.32 am	3.50 am	0–18
25	28/29	August		9.27 am	4.24 am	6–57
26	29/30	August		10.12 pm	2.55 am	4–43
27	30/31	August		9.20 pm	3.55 am	6–35
28	31/1	August		9.45 pm	3.05 am	5–20
29	1	September		10.35 pm	11.40 pm	1–5
30	2	September		12.50 am	1.50 am	1–0
31	2/3	September		10.08 pm	1.29 am	3–21
32	3	September		1.55 am	2.57 am	1–2
33	3	September		10.44 pm	11.25 pm	0–41
34	4	September		12.03 am	1.02 am	0–59
35	4/5	September		9.43 pm	3.52 am	6–9
36	5	September		9.15 am	9.30 am	0–15
37	5/6	September		10.00 pm	4.18 am	6–18
38	6	September		9.00 pm	9.30 pm	0–30
39	6	September		9.53 pm	10.35 pm	0–42
40	6/7	September		11.42 pm	2.10 am	2–28

No.	Date		Warning (or Alert)	Raiders Passed	Duration Hrs. Mins.
41	7	September	2.14 am	3.33 am	1–19
42	7/8	September	11.45 pm	3.27 am	3–42
43	9/10	September	11.40 pm	12.15 am	0–35
44	10	September	12.45 am	1.03 am	0–18
45	10/11	September	9.50 pm	1.44 am	3–54
46	11	September	12.05 pm	12.27 pm	0–22
47	11/12	September	11.00 pm	1.58 am	2–58
48	12	September	7.00 pm	7.53 pm	0–53
49	12/13	September	8.10 pm	4.07 am	7–57
50	14	September	7.58 pm	9.53 pm	1–55
51	15	September	9.27 am	9.35 am	0–8
52	15	September	8.33 pm	8.50 pm	0–17
53	15/16	September	10.42 pm	1.02 am	2–20
54	16	September	1.33 am	3.20 am	1–47
55	16	September	8.37 am	8.50 am	0–13
56	16	September	8.20 pm	9.15 pm	0–55
57	16	September	10.37 pm	11.35 pm	0–58
58	18	September	10.33 pm	11.08 pm	0–35
59	18/19	September	11.23 pm	2.05 am	2–42
60	19	September	8.55 pm	9.19 pm	0–24
61	19	September	10.29 pm	10.45 pm	0–16
62	19	September	11.23 pm	11.47 pm	0–24
63	19/20	September	11.50 pm	12.08 am	0–18
64	23	September	10.21 pm	11.21 pm	1–0
65	24	September	12.21 pm	4.35 pm	4–14
66	25	September	8.42 pm	9.27 pm	0–45
67	26	September	5.33 pm	5.46 pm	0–13
68	26/27	September	8.00 pm	1.07 am	5–7
69	27	September	1.25 am	1.50 am	0–25
70	27	September	5.35 am	5.50 am	0–15
71	27	September	7.53 pm	9.52 pm	1–59
72	28/29	September	11.47 pm	12.13 am	0–26
73	29	September	6.55 pm	7.13 pm	0–18
74	29	September	8.40 pm	9.15 pm	0–35
75	29	September	10.15 pm	11.45 pm	1–30
76	30	September	2.42 pm	3.06 pm	0–24
77	30	September	3.17 pm	3.36 pm	0–19
78	1	October	1.37 am	1.57 am	0–20
79	1/2	October	9.07 pm	12.38 am	3–31
80	2	October	5.33 am	5.52 am	0–19
81	2	October	9.26 pm	9.49 pm	0–23
82	2/3	October	10.09 pm	1.30 am	3–21
83	3	October	10.40 am	11.10 am	0–30
84	3	October	3.00 pm	3.33 pm	0–33
85	4	October	8.55 pm	9.23 pm	0–28
86	5	October	1.15 pm	1.30 pm	0–15

No.	Date		Warning (or Alert)	Raiders Passed	Duration Hrs. Mins.
87	5	October	9.00 pm	9.35 pm	0–35
88	6	October	10.10 pm	10.29 pm	0–19
89	7/8	October	8.10 pm	12.40 am	4–30
90	8	October	1.19 am	1.37 am	0–18
91	8	October	2.17 am	2.52 am	0–35
92	8	October	8.00 pm	10.00 pm	2–0
93	8	October	11.12 pm	11.43 pm	0–31
94	9	October	10.40 am	10.55 am	0–15
95	9	October	7.14 pm	7.32 pm	0–18
96	9	October	8.04 pm	10.10 pm	2–6
97	10	October	12.49 am	1.14 am	0–25
98	10	October	9.06 pm	11.35 pm	2–29
99	11	October	12.08 am	4.00 am	3–52
100	11	October	8.38 pm	11.33 pm	2–55
101	12	October	12.02 am	12.18 am	0–16
102	12	October	8.40 pm	11.00 pm	2–20
103	13	October	2.13 pm	2.37 pm	0–24
104	13	October	7.48 pm	8.03 pm	0–15
105	13	October	8.37 pm	9.21 pm	0–44
106	13/14	October	9.54 pm	12.05 am	2–11
107	14	October	12.25 am	2.30 am	2–5
108	14	October	7.14 pm	7.40 pm	0–26
109	14/15	October	8.05 pm	1.35 am	5–30
110	15	October	1.55 pm	2.20 pm	0–25
111	15/16	October	8.12 pm	4.16 am	8–4
112	16	October	8.05 pm	9.37 pm	1–32
113	17	October	3.37 pm	3.54 pm	0–17
114	17	October	7.55 pm	11.00 pm	3–5
115	18	October	7.47 pm	11.30 pm	3–43
116	19	October	12.17 pm	12.35 pm	0–18
117	19/20	October	7.47 pm	12.35 am	4–48
118	20	October	7.21 am	7.43 am	0–22
119	20	October	1.44 pm	2.05 pm	0–21
120	20	October	3.40 pm	3.49 pm	0–9
121	20/21	October	8.50 pm	5.48 am	8–58
122	21	October	10.15 am	10.30 am	0–15
123	21	October	10.49 am	11.10 am	0–21
124	21	October	11.50 am	12.30 pm	0–40
125	21	October	4.30 pm	5.00 pm	0–30
126	21/22	October	7.43 pm	12.16 am	4–33
127	22	October	11.23 am	12.03 pm	0–40
128	22	October	7.55 pm	10.30 pm	2–35
129	24	October	7.47 pm	11.15 pm	3–28
130	25	October	7.53 pm	10.55 pm	3–2
131	25	October	11.06 pm	11.15 pm	0–9
132	25	October	11.25 pm	11.45 pm	0–20

No.	Date		Warning (or Alert)	Raiders Passed	Duration Hrs. Mins.
133	25/26	October	11.50 pm	12.15 am	0–25
134	26/27	October	7.06 pm	12.20 am	5–14
135	27	October	7.00 pm	7.19 pm	0–19
136	27/28	October	8.03 pm	2.20 am	6–17
137	28	October	11.30 am	11.55 am	0–25
138	28	October	1.25 pm	1.40 pm	0–15
139	28	October	2.39 pm	3.07 pm	0–28
140	28	October	7.37 pm	11.25 pm	3–48
141	29/30	October	7.53 pm	1.37 am	5–44
142	30	October	2.58 am	4.52 am	1–54
143	30	October	11.25 am	12.15 pm	0–50
144	30	October	2.40 pm	3.08 pm	0–28
145	30	October	7.40 pm	10.00 pm	2–20
146	31	October	1.40 pm	3.32 pm	1–52
147	31	October	3.45 pm	4.24 pm	0–39
148	1	November	3.04 am	5.24 am	2–20
149	1	November	12.57 pm	1.47 pm	0–50
150	1	November	7.23 pm	9.25 pm	2–2
151	1	November	10.09 pm	11.50 pm	1–41
152	2	November	7.02 am	7.35 am	0–33
153	3	November	4.00 pm	4.58 pm	0–58
154	4	November	1.20 pm	2.07 pm	0–47
155	4	November	7.45 pm	9.25 pm	1–40
156	5	November	12.42 am	2.25 am	1–43
157	5	November	7.11 pm	7.37 pm	0–26
158	5	November	10.35 pm	11.50 pm	1–15
159	6	November	12.18 am	2.04 am	1–46
160	6	November	3.45 am	4.45 am	1–0
161	6	November	9.05 pm	9.32 pm	0–27
162	6/7	November	10.35 pm	12.07 am	1–32
163	7	November	7.38 pm	9.09 pm	1–31
164	7	November	10.33 pm	11.08 pm	0–35
165	7/8	November	11.55 pm	12.45 am	0–50
166	8	November	12.35 pm	1.03 pm	0–28
167	8	November	7.10 pm	11.38 pm	4–28
168	9	November	12.00 am	1.13 pm	1–13
169	9	November	3.20 pm	4.09 pm	0–49
170	9	November	7.03 pm	8.35 pm	1–32
171	10	November	6.58 pm	11.46 pm	4–48
172	11	November	2.40 am	2.55 am	0–15
173	11	November	12.00 am	12.27 pm	0–27
174	11	November	3.19 pm	3.53 pm	0–34
175	12	November	8.48 pm	11.50 pm	3–2
176	13	November	12.18 am	12.37 am	0–19
177	13	November	12.45 pm	2.22 pm	1–37
178	13	November	4.05 pm	5.00 pm	0–55

No.	Date		Warning (or Alert)	Raiders Passed	Duration Hrs. Mins.
179	14	November	9.45 am	10.15 am	0–30
180	14/15	November	7.05 pm	6.16 am	11–11
181	15	November	4.00 pm	4.40 pm	0–40
182	15	November	6.35 pm	11.57 pm	5–22
183	16	November	1.10 am	1.30 am	0–20
184	16	November	3.11 am	6.38 am	3–27
185	16	November	7.43 pm	8.01 pm	0–18
186	16	November	11.32 pm	11.45 pm	0–13
187	17	November	2.45 pm	3.14 pm	0–29
188	17	November	10.05 pm	10.46 pm	0–41
189	18	November	8.16 pm	11.14 pm	2–58
190	18/19	November	11.32 pm	5.03 am	5–31
191	19/20	November	6.50 pm	4.28 am	9–38
192	20	November	12.25 pm	12.45 pm	0–20
193	20/21	November	7.28 pm	6.23 am	10–55
194	21	November	10.14 am	10.31 am	0–17
195	21	November	2.20 pm	2.32 pm	0–12
196	21	November	7.30 pm	9.42 pm	2–12
197	22	November	10.45 am	11.22 am	0–37
198	22	November	12.30 pm	12.50 pm	0–20
199	22	November	3.40 pm	4.30 pm	0–50
200	22/23	November	6.40 pm	5.47 am	11–7
201	23	November	1.09 pm	2.45 pm	1–36
202	23	November	8.20 pm	9.00 pm	0–40
203	24	November	11.30 am	12.25 pm	0–55
204	24	November	8.00 pm	9.19 pm	1–19
205	26	November	3.20 pm	4.03 pm	0–43
206	26	November	10.15 pm	10.57 pm	0–42
207	28	November	4.15 pm	4.42 pm	0–27
208	28/29	November	6.55 pm	4.07 am	9–12
209	29	November	10.43 pm	10.56 pm	0–13
210	1	December	7.30 pm	8.44 pm	1–14
211	2	December	6.33 pm	6.58 pm	0–25
212	3	December	3.02 pm	3.15 pm	0–13
213	3	December	6.20 pm	10.30 pm	4–10
214	4	December	1.42 pm	2.02 pm	0–20
215	4	December	2.10 pm	2.55 pm	0–45
216	4	December	3.50 pm	4.20 pm	0–30
217	4	December	6.55 pm	10.15 pm	3–20
218	5	December	7.20 am	8.00 am	0–40
219	5	December	8.13 am	8.37 am	0–24
220	5	December	2.40 pm	3.28 pm	0–48
221	6	December	7.20 pm	9.07 pm	1–47
222	6	December	9.40 pm	10.44 pm	1–4
223	7	December	11.45 am	12.15 pm	0–30
224	9	December	1.20 pm	1.35 pm	0–15

No.	Date			Warning (or Alert)	Raiders Passed	Duration Hrs. Mins.
225	11/12	December		6.28 pm	1.32 am	7–4
226	12	December		1.45 am	2.00 am	0–15
227	12	December		2.39 am	7.37 am	4–58
228	12	December		1.13 pm	1.30 pm	0–17
229	12/13	December		7.05 pm	4.27 am	9–22
230	14	December		4.55 pm	5.31 pm	0–36
231	15	December		1.20 pm	1.37 pm	0–17
232	15	December		6.25 pm	10.19 pm	3–54
233	16	December		2.20 pm	2.45 pm	0–25
234	16	December		8.10 pm	9.32 pm	1–22
235	17	December		1.48 pm	2.45 pm	0–57
236	19	December		1.15 pm	1.30 pm	0–15
237	20/21	December		6.14 pm	1.45 am	7–31
238	21/22	December		6.16 pm	3.35 am	9–19
239	22/23	December		6.20 pm	4.47 am	10–27
240	23	December		3.55 pm	4.30 pm	0–35
241	23/24	December		6.40 pm	1.28 am	6–48
242	28	December		3.20 pm	3.35 pm	0–15
243	29	December		3.45 pm	3.53 pm	0–8
244	1/2	January	1941	8.24 pm	12.32 am	4–8
245	2	January		1.02 am	1.46 am	0–44
246	2	January		2.15 am	2.45 am	0–30
247	2	January		4.45 am	7.07 am	2–22
248	2	January		9.35 pm	10.47 pm	1–12
249	3	January		9.22 pm	10.24 pm	1–2
250	4/5	January		10.45 pm	2.29 am	3–44
251	5	January		4.35 am	6.43 am	2–8
252	7	January		1.25 pm	2.15 pm	0–50
253	7	January		4.55 pm	5.30 pm	0–35
254	8	January		2.55 pm	3.25 pm	0–30
255	9/10	January		7.15 pm	1.47 am	6–32
256	10	January		4.15 pm	4.30 pm	0–15
257	10	January		7.15 pm	7.34 pm	0–19
258	15	January		7.32 pm	8.07 pm	0–35
259	15/16	January		8.58 pm	1.21 am	4–23
260	16	January		3.17 am	5.07 am	1–50
261	17	January		2.38 pm	2.50 pm	0–12
262	17	January		4.55 pm	5.10 pm	0–15
263	17	January		9.37 pm	10.19 pm	0–42
264	19	January		9.12 pm	9.21 pm	0–9
265	21	January		3.12 pm	3.56 pm	0–44
266	26	January		8.35 pm	8.50 pm	0–15
267	3	February		10.40 pm	10.48 pm	0–8
268	4	February		7.32 pm	11.00 pm	3–28
269	5	February		11.00 pm	11.12 pm	0–12
270	6	February		12.30 pm	1.20 pm	0–50

No.	Date		Warning (or Alert)	Raiders Passed	Duration Hrs. Mins.
271	12	February	6.35 am	7.15 am	0–40
272	12	February	3.00 pm	3.46 pm	0–46
273	15	February	2.47 pm	3.12 pm	0–25
274	15/16	February	11.08 pm	2.31 am	3–23
275	16	February	12.29 pm	1.15 pm	0–46
276	19	February	2.10 pm	2.51 pm	0–41
277	19	February	9.24 pm	9.44 pm	0–20
278	20	February	8.39 pm	9.00 pm	0–21
279	21	February	11.15 pm	11.51 pm	0–36
280	24	February	2.50 pm	3.06 pm	0–16
281	26	February	8.34 pm	9.25 pm	0–51
282	27	February	12.32 pm	12.50 pm	0–18
283	27	February	2.10 pm	2.27 pm	0–17
284	1	March	8.45 pm	10.03 pm	1–18
285	3	March	9.55 pm	11.42 pm	1–47
286	4	March	12.47 am	1.02 am	0–15
287	5	March	3.10 pm	3.25 pm	0–15
288	7	March	12.35 pm	12.55 pm	0–20
289	7	March	3.35 pm	4.25 pm	0–50
290	9	March	8.25 pm	9.33 pm	1–8
291	11/12	March	8.35 pm	12.07 am	3–32
292	12	March	8.23 pm	11.50 pm	3–27
293	13/14	March	8.56 pm	3.28 am	6–32
294	14/15	March	8.30 pm	1.53 am	5–23
295	15	March	9.30 pm	10.00 pm	0–30
296	17	March	12.10 am	12.29 am	0–19
297	18	March	10.10 pm	11.18 pm	1–8
298	21/22	March	11.47 pm	12.30 am	0–43
299	23	March	12.05 pm	12.15 pm	0–10
300	26	March	12.20 pm	12.32 pm	0–12
301	26	March	3.55 pm	4.15 pm	0–20
302	29	March	9.25 pm	9.58 pm	0–33
303	3	April	11.17 pm	11.56 pm	0–39
304	7/8	April	9.25 pm	4.00 am	6–35
305	8/9	April	9.54 pm	5.15 am	7–21
306	9/10	April	9.33 pm	2.48 am	5–15
307	10/11	April	9.40 pm	3.26 am	5–46
308	15	April	2.47 pm	3.30 pm	0–43
309	15/16	April	10.57 pm	4.07 am	5–10
310	22	April	11.06 pm	11.51 pm	0–45
311	26	April	6.43 pm	6.59 pm	0–16
312	26/27	April	10.00 pm	1.55 am	3–55
313	30	April	11.00 am	11.20 am	0–20
314	1/2	May	10.32 pm	12.50 am	2–18
315	2/3	May	10.04 pm	1.54 am	3–50
316	3/4	May	10.57 pm(BST)	5.34 am(BDST)	5–37

No.	Date			Warning (or Alert)	Raiders Passed	Duration Hrs. Mins.
317	4/5	May		11.45 pm	4.12 am	4–27
318	6	May		3.12 am	4.02 am	0–50
319	6/7	May		11.27 pm	4.12 am	4–45
320	8	May		12.26 am	3.00 am	2–34
321	8/9	May		11.43 pm	3.25 am	3–42
322	9/10	May		11.50 pm	2.30 am	2–40
323	11	May		12.07 am	1.27 am	1–20
324	17	May		12.15 am	4.25 am	4–10
325	29	May		2.07 am	2.50 am	0–43
326	31	May		1.50 am	3.20 am	1–30
327	1	June		12.28 am	2.49 am	2–21
328	2	June		1.10 am	3.35 am	2–25
329	5/6	June		12.35 am	3.13 am	2–38
330	12	June		12.35 am	3.47 am	3–12
331	13	June		12.35 pm	1.34 pm	0–59
332	15	June		1.08 am	1.33 am	0–25
333	17	June		1.03 am	2.15 am	1–12
334	24	June		2.00 am	2.28 am	0–28
335	5	July		1.15 am	3.35 am	2–20
336	9	July		1.07 am	3.33 am	2–26
337	14	July		1.55 pm	2.10 pm	0–15
338	12/13	August		11.52 pm	1.40 am	1–48
339	18	August		11.15 pm	11.25 pm	0–10
340	22	October		9.07 pm	11.25 pm	2–18
341	1	November		9.05 pm	11.04 pm	1–59
342	18	December		7.32 pm	7.46 pm	0–14
343	29	December		8.57 pm	9.10 pm	0–13
344	10/11	January	1942	11.43 pm	1.17 am	1–34
345	2	March		4.28 pm	5.18 pm	0–50
346	18	April		3.15 am	3.38 am	0–23
347	26	April		4.50 am	5.20 am	0–30
348	25	June		1.05 am	2.30 am	1–25
349	16	July		6.15 am	6.30 am	0–15
350	23/24	July		11.55 pm	12.58 am	1–3
351	27	July		6.15 am	7.22 am	1–7
352	27	July		8.00 am	8.27 am	0–27
353	28	July		1.42 am	3.59 am	2–17
354	30	July		1.28 am	4.05 am	2–37
355	31	July		1.03 am	3.22 am	2–19
356	3	August		2.55 am	3.28 am	0–33
357	3	August		1.55 pm	2.15 pm	0–20
358	8	August		1.00 am	1.25 am	0–25
359	8	August		6.02 pm	6.33 pm	0–31
360	12	August		1.52 am	2.17 am	0–25
361	23	August		10.30 pm	11.21 pm	0–51
362	5	September		11.30 am	12.00 am	0–30

No.	Date			Warning (or Alert)	Raiders Passed	Duration Hrs. Mins.
363	6	September		4.15 pm	4.28 pm	0–13
364	4	March	1943	9.15 am	9.45 am	0–30
365	23	April		10.58 pm	11.25 pm	0–27
366	5	June		12.20 am	12.48 am	0–28
367	4	February	1944	5.35 am	5.50 am	0–15
368	23	February		12.30 am	1.04 am	0–34
369	25	March		12.29 am	1.00 am	0–31
370	27/28	March		11.57 pm	12.20 am	0–23
371	21	April		12.25 am	12.47 am	0–22
372	24	December		5.35 am	6.28 am	0–53
373	4	March	1945	1.15 am	1.50 am	0–35
						675–13

Wardens who were attached to Post E.24A in November, 1940

J. V. Abbott, L. Bailey, Baker, G. E. Barrett, (Miss) A. Bellamy, P. C. Biddle, F. J. Blackband, A. J. Bott, Brindley, R. J. Brown, H. G. Brunt, Bull, P. F. Burt, A. L. Cadman, (Miss) J. Carradine, R. A. Corfield, H. G. Couch, C. Cox, J. H. Cracknell, G. V. W. Darby, C. H. Deeming, J. Dennis, A. H. Duffill, J. Eite, R. C. Elwell, R. Evans, T. F. Fearn, S. G. Foster, H. Giles, F. J. Godfree, C. H. Greaves, (Mrs) F. M. Greaves, W. Hackney, G. J. Hall, L. T. J. Hands, Harman, T. N. Harris, A. V. Harrison, F. E. Hartley, (Mrs) Hartley, H. S. Hawcutt, A. Hayward (Messenger), E. J. Hewitt, N. Holland, (Mrs) G. W. Hookway, N. J. Hookway, S. Humphries, C. A. Hunt, (Mrs) D. M. Hyde, Jacques, A. E. Jackson, Jennings, H. A. Johnson, J. H. Johnson, H. Keates, F. Knight, J. G. Law, (Mrs) I. M. Lyons, Madge, W. H. Meadows, Marles, J. Michell, W. J. Miles, E. Miller, T. A. Milner, E. T. Nelson, (Miss) L. Osborne, B. J. Page, T. B. Partington, G. Perks, G. Preston, (Mrs) G. Preston, (Mrs) I. K. Price, L. J. Price, F. A. Purser, A. J. Reeves, G. W. Reynolds, F. E. F. Rowley, B. D. Sanders, H. H. Sanders, H. W. Shotton, B. J. Smith, R. H. Smith, R. B. Spence, C. Taylor, C. J. Taylor, E. Taylor, H. E. Taylor, P. Taylor, (Mrs) R. E. Taylor, (Mrs) R. M. Taylor, E. Tew, (Mrs) E. W. Thomas, H. E. Thomas, (Mrs) A. G. Titterton, W. J. Titterton, Toye, (Mrs) Toye, E. A. Tullett, (Mrs) M. E. M. Tullett, J. H. Turner, (Mrs) Wagstaffe, C. J. Wall, E. R. Watson, G. B. Webb, A. C. Wetten, C. C. Whitehead, J. E. Williams, E. E. Wilson, E. W. Wilson, L. T. Windmill, E. Wood, J. C. Wright.

Incidents reported from E. 24A

Date			Number	Total
16	August	1940	6	6
24	August	1940	1	7
26/27	August	1940	1	8
3	September	1940	5	13
22	October	1940	18	31
25/26	October	1940	1	32
8	November	1940	1	33
19/20	November	1940	3	36
20/21	November	1940	1	37
22/23	November	1940	9	46
11	December	1940	1	47
9/10	April	1941	4	51
17	May	1941	10	61
30	July	1942	1	62
31	July	1942	21	83

Our Warden (November, 1940)

Who walks the street at dead of night?
Who shouts, 'Put out that blooming light!'?
Who waits for 'Red' to change to 'White'?
Our Warden!

When things go hurtling through night's space,
Who throws himself upon his face?
Who thinks he's in that red hot place?
Our Warden!

Who never goes upstairs to bed?
Who braves the elements instead?
Who walks about as if half dead?
Our Warden!

Who says, 'Stay put, I will not quit'?
Whose uniform is one misfit?
Who takes good care he won't get hit?
Our Warden!

Who listens out for every sound?
Who tucks his neighbours underground?
Who looks for bombs that can't be found?
Our Warden!

Who whistles loud when sirens shriek?
Who shouts so loud, he cannot speak?
Who binds his knees because they're weak?
Our Warden!

Who just makes shift with what will do,
The rubbing rag for all and few?
Who's errand boy and nurse-maid too?
Our Warden!

Who says he means to see it through?
Who'd stop for months within a queue,
To help to cut 'that man' in two?
Our Warden!

J.V.A.

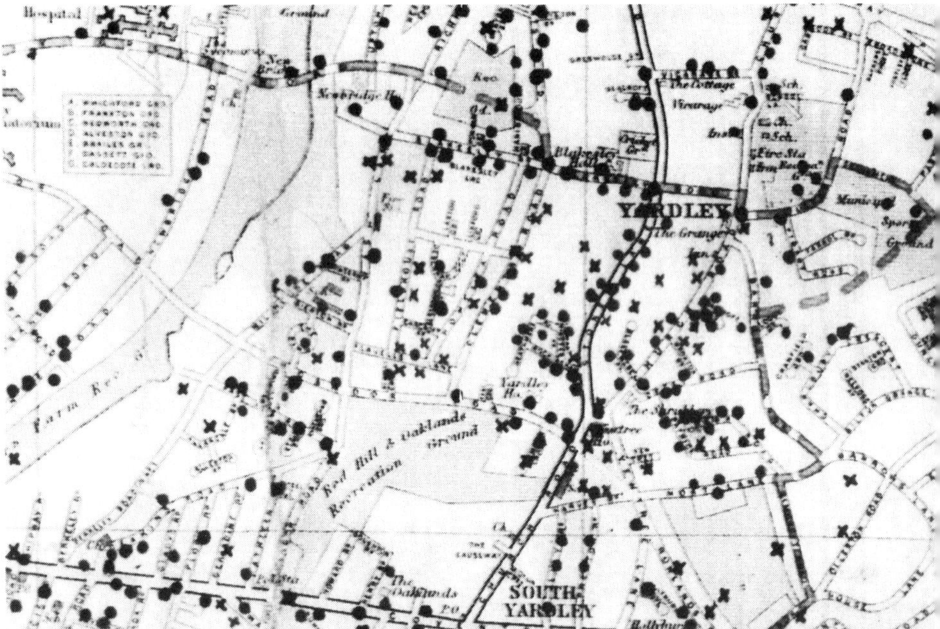

Hospital
YARDLEY
The Cottage
Vicarage
Red Hill & Oaklands
Recreation Ground
SOUTH
YARDLEY
HAY MILLS
CEMETERY
Highfield Fm.
STOCKFIELD
Wharf
Farm
Isolation
Hospital

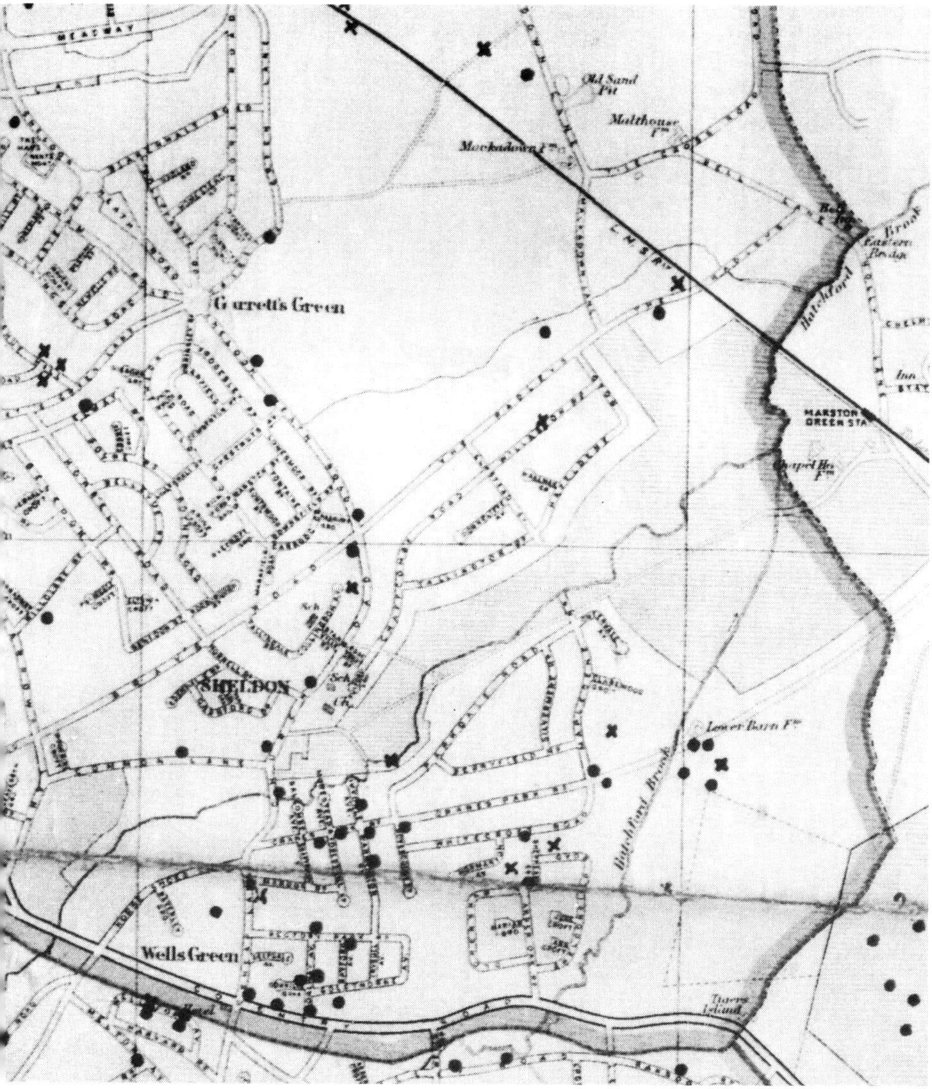

Old Sand Pit
Malthouse Fm
Garrett's Green
MARSTON GREEN STA
Inn
SHELDON
Lower Barn Fm
Hatchford Brook
Wells Green

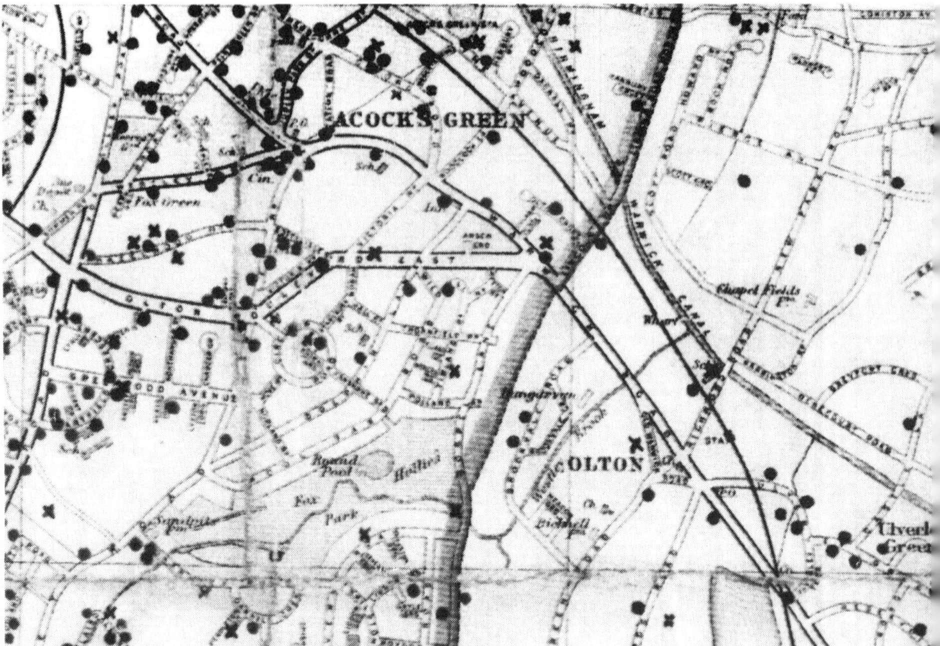
ACOCK'S GREEN
Fox Green
OLTON
Round Pool
Fox Park
Chapel Fields Fm
Hineton Green
Mereside
Langley Hall Farm
St Bernards Grange
Arden Vale
Franciscan Monastery
Bathing Pool
Stretton Farm
Oak Cottage
Golf Course
Woodfield

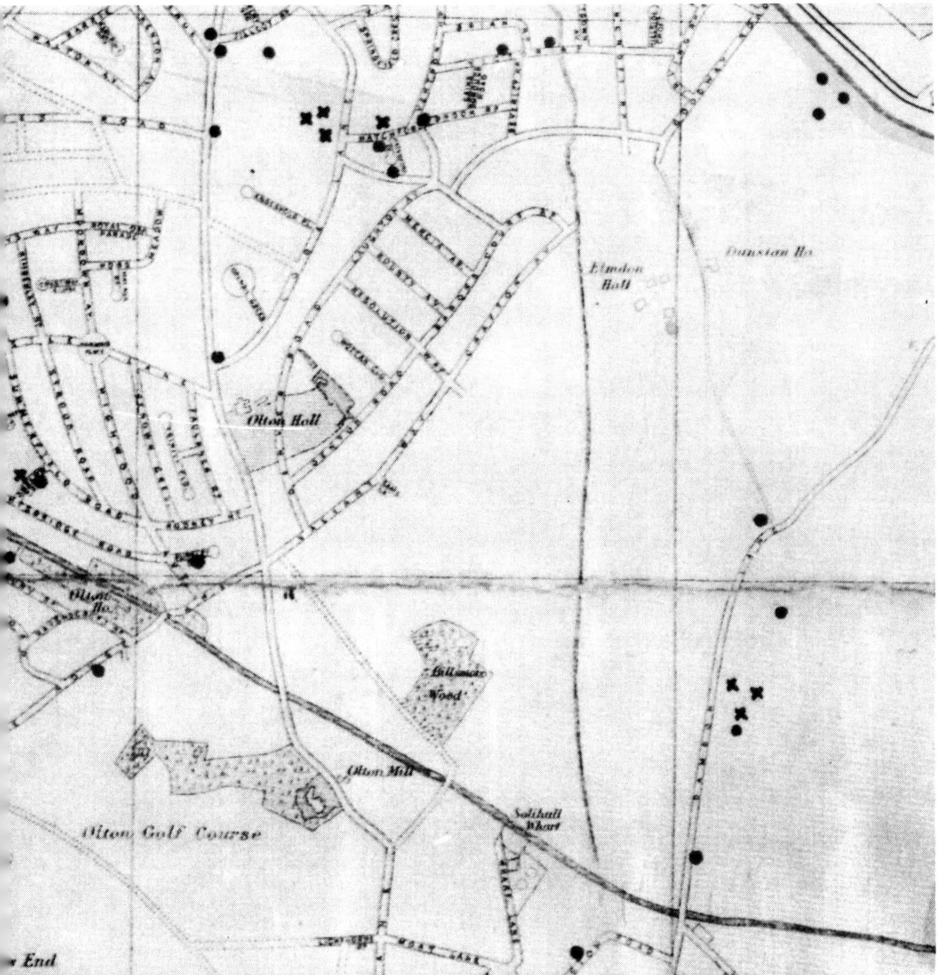
Dunstan Ho
Elmdon Hall
Olton Hall
Olton Mill
Solihall Wharf
Olton Golf Course
Elmdon Heath
End